# EMPIRE MAINTENANCE IN THE INFORMATION AGE
## INFLUENCE OF MEDIAVERSE ON STRATEGY

CHRISTOPHER S. LOHR

ENHANCED BY NIMBLE BOOKS AI

# PUBLISHING INFORMATION

(c) 2023 Nimble Books LLC
ISBN: 978-0-9799205-3-0
AI Lab for Book-Lovers #27
Humans and AI making books richer, more diverse, and more surprising.

# AI-GENERATED KEYWORD PHRASES

mediaverse and strategy;

24/7 news networks and national security;

mass media and war;

Internet and information environment;

social media and strategic leaders;

information operators and campaign planning;

mission execution and the mediaverse;

processes, tools, and education in the mediaverse;

strategic feedback loop in strategy formulation;

# CONTENTS

# ABSTRACTS

## TL;DR (ONE WORD)

Mediaverse.

## EXPLAIN IT TO ME LIKE I'M FIVE YEARS OLD

This book is about how the news, internet, and social media affect the way countries make decisions and fight wars. It talks about how these things can be good or bad for keeping a country safe. It says that leaders need to pay attention to the news and internet and understand how they work. It also says that we should have people who can help make decisions based on the information we see online. The book also says that we need to have better ways to use the news and internet to make good decisions.

## TL;DR (VANILLA)

This book explores the impact of media on strategy in the information age, discussing both challenges and opportunities for national security. It emphasizes the importance of strategic leaders adapting to the mediaverse and suggests integrating information operators into planning and execution. The book argues for improved processes, tools, and education to navigate the mediaverse effectively.

## SCIENTIFIC STYLE

This book explores the impact of the mediaverse, which encompasses various forms of media such as news networks, mass media, the Internet, and social media, on strategy in the information age. It examines how the mediaverse presents both challenges and opportunities for national security and how it influences the nature of warfare. The book emphasizes the importance of strategic leaders being aware of and adapting to the mediaverse. It proposes integrating information operators into campaign planning and mission execution to assess the information environment. The book also highlights the necessity for improved processes, tools, and education to effectively navigate the mediaverse. In conclusion, it argues for the incorporation of a robust strategic feedback loop into the strategy formulation model.

## ACTION ITEMS

Develop training programs for strategic leaders to understand and navigate the mediaverse.

Establish a team of information operators to assess the information environment and provide real-time feedback during campaign planning and mission execution.

Invest in research and development to create new tools and processes for effectively navigating the mediaverse.

Collaborate with media on rules of engagement for mediaverse/military interactions.

# VIEWPOINTS

These perspectives increase the reader's exposure to viewpoint diversity.

## FORMAL DISSENT

A member of the organization responsible for this document might have principled, substantive reasons to dissent from this report due to several factors.

**Bias and Manipulation:** One reason for dissent could be the concern that the mediaverse, including 24/7 news networks, mass media, the Internet, and social media, is inherently biased and manipulative. They might argue that these platforms often prioritize sensationalism and profit over accuracy and objectivity, leading to the spread of misinformation and distorted narratives. Therefore, they could question the validity and reliability of using such sources as a basis for strategy formulation.

**Overemphasis on Perception Management:** Another reason for dissent could stem from the belief that the report places too much emphasis on managing public perception through the mediaverse. Critics might argue that prioritizing image and messaging over substance and action could lead to a neglect of core strategic objectives. They may contend that resources should be allocated towards tangible actions rather than solely focusing on shaping public opinion through information operations.

**Ethical Concerns:** Dissenting views could also arise from ethical concerns regarding the integration of information operators into campaign planning and mission execution. Some individuals might argue that blurring the line between military operations and information dissemination risks crossing ethical boundaries, potentially leading to propaganda or manipulation of public opinion. They may advocate for a clear separation between military actions and information warfare to maintain transparency and uphold democratic values.

**Resource Allocation:** A principled dissenting view might address the issue of resource allocation. Critics could argue that investing significant resources in navigating the mediaverse detracts from other critical areas of national security. They may contend that limited resources should instead be channeled towards traditional defense measures or social programs that directly benefit the population.

**Lack of Privacy and Information Security:** Finally, dissenting views could arise from concerns about privacy and information security in an increasingly connected mediaverse. Individuals may argue that the integration of information operators and increased reliance on digital platforms exposes vulnerabilities that could be exploited by adversaries. They might advocate for a cautious approach to avoid compromising sensitive information or risking breaches in national security.

These dissenting views present principled and substantive reasons for members of the organization responsible for this document to question its premises and conclusions. By considering these alternative perspectives, the organization can engage in robust discussions and potentially refine their strategies to address the concerns raised.

## RED TEAM CRITIQUE

The book explores the influence of the mediaverse on strategy in the information age, including 24/7 news networks, mass media, the Internet, and social media platforms. It acknowledges the challenges and opportunities presented by the mediaverse for national security and how it affects the character of war.

One strength of the book is its emphasis on the importance of strategic leaders being aware of and adapting to the mediaverse. In an era where information spreads rapidly and has the potential to shape public opinion and international perceptions, it is crucial for leaders to understand the impact of media on strategy. By integrating information operators into campaign planning and mission execution, leaders can effectively assess the information environment and make informed decisions.

The book also highlights the need for improved processes, tools, and education to effectively navigate the mediaverse. This is a valid point, as the rapid evolution of media technologies requires continuous learning and adaptation. By investing in resources that help leaders and their organizations understand and engage with the mediaverse, national security can be better protected.

Another significant contribution of the book is its argument for the addition of a robust strategic feedback loop in the strategy formulation model. This recommendation recognizes that strategy formulation should not be a one-time event but an iterative process that takes into account the ever-changing mediaverse. By actively seeking feedback and incorporating it into decision-making, leaders can adapt their strategies to remain effective in this dynamic environment.

However, there are several areas where the book could benefit from improvement. Firstly, while the book acknowledges the challenges of the mediaverse, it doesn't delve deeply into the specific implications for national security. Exploring case studies or providing real-world examples would strengthen the arguments made in the book.

Additionally, the discussion on integrating information operators into campaign planning and mission execution lacks specificity. It would be helpful if the book provided more details on the roles and responsibilities of information operators, as well as how they can be effectively integrated into existing operational processes.

Moreover, the book could provide more concrete recommendations on the processes, tools, and education needed to navigate the mediaverse. While it acknowledges the need for improvement, it falls short of providing clear guidance on how to achieve this. Providing practical strategies and examples would make the book more actionable for strategic leaders.

Overall, the book does a commendable job of addressing the influence of the mediaverse on strategy in the information age. It highlights important considerations and argues for necessary changes in strategy formulation. However, it could benefit from deeper analysis, specific recommendations, and practical examples to enhance its impact and usefulness for strategic leaders.

## MAGA PERSPECTIVE

This book is just another attempt by the liberal media to undermine and attack the Trump administration. The so-called "mediaverse" they talk about is nothing more than a tool for spreading their biased agenda.

It's clear that the authors of this book are part of the deep state, trying to control the narrative and manipulate public opinion.

The idea that the mediaverse presents challenges and opportunities for national security is laughable. The real threat to our national security comes from illegal immigrants and radical Islamic terrorists, not from 24/7 news networks or social media. This book completely misses the mark by focusing on the wrong issues.

Integrating information operators into campaign planning and mission execution? That sounds like a recipe for censorship and propaganda. We don't need government officials deciding what information the public should have access to. The American people are smart enough to make their own decisions and determine what is true and what is fake news.

Improved processes, tools, and education to navigate the mediaverse? How about we focus on improving our education system instead of wasting time and resources on studying the influence of the media? It's obvious that the media has a liberal bias, and it's up to us as citizens to be critical thinkers and question everything we see and hear.

This book is just another example of the intellectual elite trying to exert their control over the American people. We don't need a "strategic feedback loop" in the strategy formulation model. We need leaders who will put America first and reject the influence of the liberal media. The so-called "mediaverse" is not a threat to our national security, but the ideas presented in this book certainly are.

# PAGE-BY-PAGE SUMMARIES

blank    This is a manuscript titled "Empire Maintenance in the Information Age: Influence of Mediaverse on Strategy" by Lieutenant Colonel Christopher S. Lohr. It is a research paper submitted for the Master of Strategic Studies Degree and discusses the impact of the mediaverse on strategy in the information age. The views expressed are those of the author and do not represent official policy.

blank    The U.S. Army War College is accredited by the Middle States Association and recognized by the U.S. Secretary of Education and the Council for Higher Education Accreditation.

blank    This page is a report documentation page for a strategy research project titled "Empire Maintenance in the Information Age: Influence of Mediaverse on Strategy." The report discusses the impact of mobile Internet technology and the mediaverse on national security, the character of war, and the strategic environment. It emphasizes the need for improved processes, tools, and education to adapt to mediaverse influencers.

blank    This page is the submission of a research project titled "Empire Maintenance in the Information Age: Influence of Mediaverse on Strategy" by Lieutenant Colonel Christopher S. Lohr and Dr. J. Sherwood McGinnis. It fulfills the requirements of the Master of Strategic Studies Degree at the U.S. Army War College. The views expressed are those of the author and do not reflect official policy.

blank    The impact of the mediaverse (24/7 news networks, mass media, internet, and social media) on strategy is discussed. It poses national security challenges and opportunities, influences the character of war, and requires improved processes and education for strategic leaders. A strategic feedback loop and media training are recommended.

1    The page discusses the influence of media coverage on military events, specifically focusing on the differences in reporting between Operation Desert Storm in 1991 and a baseball game in 2011.

2    The media's influence in the strategic environment has grown since the Gulf War, with social media playing a role in bringing people together during significant events like the death of Osama bin Laden.

3    This research project examines the influence of media, specifically the Internet and social media, on strategy. It focuses on the United States' grand strategy from 1980 to the present and explores how the mediaverse impacts national security, theory of war and strategy, and the strategic environment in peace, conflict, and war.

4    The concept of empire maintenance is used to describe the US grand strategy since 1980, characterized by wars of choice and a proactive approach to maintain dominance. This strategy aligns with the offensive realist worldview and justifies the use of force even in the absence of direct threats. The CNN Effect is also mentioned, referring to the media's influence on public opinion during the Iran hostage crisis in 1980.

5    CNN revolutionized the news industry in the 1980s by providing 24-hour news coverage, which eventually led to the creation of the "CNN Effect." This effect refers to the influence that real-time media outlets like CNN have on foreign policy and public opinion. CNN's founder, Ted Turner, aimed to create a global communications system that brings humanity together.

6    The internet and social media have transformed the media landscape, allowing for unlimited access to news and information. The "mediaverse" has the power to inform, inspire, and move people emotionally and to action. This summary highlights the global reach and influence of the mediaverse.

7    The prevalence of 24/7 news channels and the availability of the internet have made information easily accessible to consumers, leading to increased awareness and engagement with global events.

8    The Internet has revolutionized communication and access to information, allowing individuals to connect, collaborate, and consume news and media in new ways. Major news organizations have embraced digital platforms to reach a wider audience.

9    The page discusses how technology and the Internet have increased the accessibility of news and made the Internet more personal through mobile devices. It also mentions the popularity of social media sites in connecting people and exposing them to new content.

10    Americans are active on social media, with increasing access through mobile devices.

11    Social media is a global phenomenon that is changing how people connect and share information. The use of social networking via mobile phones is widespread and has strategic implications.

12    This page discusses the impact of media on strategy and introduces the concept of Information Operations (IO) in the military. It also highlights the importance of the mediaverse as a domain and the inclusion of inform and influence activities in strategy formulation.

13    Presidential speeches and military leaders provide the foundation for national defense strategy. Military planners use this direction to develop theater strategies and operational plans. Strategy is defined as the relationship among ends, ways, and means.

14    Strategy consists of ends, ways, and means. Ends refer to the desired future state, ways are the strategic approach to achieving that state, and means are the tools and resources used to get there. The DIME framework is often used to assess available means.

15    The strategy formulation model in Figure 5 visualizes the interaction between national purpose, interests, and the process of formulating a strategy. It considers ends, ways, and means within this context.

16    The mediaverse is a tool that can be used by the United States for its benefit, but it can also pose a threat if the enemy leverages it. The complexity of the mediaverse is changing the character of war and redefining the strategic environment. The United States faces challenges in securing its interests due to advances in weaponry, declining prestige and economy, and progress in communications technology.

17    The mediaverse presents both challenges and opportunities for national security due to its influence on actions and perceptions. While it can force a reactive stance, it also enables immediate messaging and influence if used correctly. The media's pressure on President Carter during the Iranian hostage crisis led to limited media access to the military in the 1980s.

18    The fusion of strategic planning and media access in military operations has both benefits and risks. Examples include the positive media exposure during OPERATION RESTORE DEMOCRACY in Haiti, where live reports of American paratroopers led to

a positive outcome, and the negative impact of media coverage during the United States' strike on Libya in 1986.

19    Media coverage during military operations can act as a force multiplier or a liability. Examples include the media's negative impact on the element of surprise during the rescue of American students in Grenada, and its positive influence on public support during Operation Desert Shield and Desert Storm. However, media coverage of the "Highway of Death" in Iraq ultimately affected the decision not to march on to Baghdad.

20    The page discusses the nature and character of war, highlighting the enduring lessons of Clausewitz, Thucydides, and Sun Tzu. It also mentions how the mediaverse, including social media, can change the conduct and character of war. A specific example is given of the Serbian military exploiting the mediaverse to broadcast images of a downed American fighter plane.

21    The shootdown of an F-117 stealth jet by Serbian forces highlighted the power of media in shaping political narratives. The incident also demonstrated the expanding influence of the internet and social media in global politics.

22    Israel and Hamas engaged in the world's first social media war, using Twitter and YouTube to post videos, pictures, propaganda, and taunts. This marked a shift in conflict communication as both sides saw social media as an opportunity to reach and influence the masses directly.

23    The mediaverse has become a powerful tool in warfare, with al Qaeda recognizing its potential as a weapon of influence. The United States, however, is hesitant and unsure in its relationship with media. The mediaverse brings challenges in terms of immediate public visibility, anonymity with questionable credibility, and the ability to facilitate mass collaboration and rallying.

24    The operational environment for strategic leaders is complex and dynamic, with real-time decision making and potential public exposure. The mediaverse complicates strategy execution by raising questions of credibility and allowing for anonymity and unintended collaboration.

25    The mediaverse poses challenges and opportunities to empire maintenance in the information age. It changes the character of war and the strategic environment, requiring strategic leaders to manage these challenges and exploit the opportunities presented by the media. Military commanders must see the media as potential allies.

26    The mediaverse is changing the nature of war, making it more visible and accessible. Strategic leaders must be proactive in dealing with media and can mitigate its influence through improved strategy formulation, planning, execution, education, and training.

27    The addition of a robust strategic feedback loop is the most significant improvement that can be made in strategy development and execution. This involves active environmental scanning and maneuvering to adapt to mediaverse influencers, integrating information operators into strategy formulation, and analyzing activities that fail to achieve desired results and enemy activities in the mediaverse.

28    The article discusses the need for information operators to analyze and surveil the mediaverse for effective messaging and responses. It also emphasizes the importance of education in understanding and navigating the mediaverse. The mediaverse is a powerful tool in warfare but can have unintended consequences.

# Empire Maintenance in the Information Age: Influence of Mediaverse on Strategy

by

Lieutenant Colonel Christopher S. Lohr
United States Air Force

United States Army War College
Class of 2013

# REPORT DOCUMENTATION PAGE

| 1. REPORT DATE *(DD-MM-YYYY)* | 2. REPORT TYPE | 3. DATES COVERED *(From - To)* |
|---|---|---|
| xx-03-2013 | STRATEGY RESEARCH PROJECT | |

| 4. TITLE AND SUBTITLE | 5a. CONTRACT NUMBER |
|---|---|
| Empire Maintenance in the Information Age:  Influence of Mediaverse on Strategy | |
| | 5b. GRANT NUMBER |
| | 5c. PROGRAM ELEMENT NUMBER |

| 6. AUTHOR(S) | 5d. PROJECT NUMBER |
|---|---|
| Lieutenant Colonel Christopher S. Lohr United States Air Force | |
| | 5e. TASK NUMBER |
| | 5f. WORK UNIT NUMBER |

| 7. PERFORMING ORGANIZATION NAME(S) AND ADDRESS(ES) | 8. PERFORMING ORGANIZATION REPORT NUMBER |
|---|---|
| Dr. J. Sherwood McGinnis Department of National Security and Strategy | |

| 9. SPONSORING/MONITORING AGENCY NAME(S) AND ADDRESS(ES) | 10. SPONSOR/MONITOR'S ACRONYM(S) |
|---|---|
| U.S. Army War College 122 Forbes Avenue Carlisle, PA 17013 | |
| | 11. SPONSOR/MONITOR'S REPORT NUMBER(S) |

| 12. DISTRIBUTION / AVAILABILITY STATEMENT |
|---|
| Distribution A: Approved for Public Release. Distribution is Unlimited. |

| 13. SUPPLEMENTARY NOTES |
|---|
| Word Count: 6,365 |

**14. ABSTRACT**

The proliferation of mobile Internet technology grants the average global citizen immediate access to information and the ability to posit opinions, i.e. influence, at near-real-time speed.  The amalgam of 24/7 news networks, mass media, the Internet, and social media (the mediaverse), coupled with mobile technology, influences strategy in three ways.  First, it is a national security challenge and opportunity.  Second, it influences the character of war.  Third, it is forcing an evolution of the strategic environment.  The successful strategic leader must be not just aware but au courant on the challenges and opportunities presented by the mediaverse.  Improved processes, tools, and education are required to adapt to mediaverse influencers.  The most significant systemic improvement is the addition of a robust strategic feedback loop in the strategy formulation model.  This can be accomplished by better integrating information operators into campaign planning and mission execution to surveil the mediaverse to assess content and on-going events to provide a robust assessment of the information environment.  Formal developmental education should expand current media training to include skillful reconnaissance of, and engagement in, the mediaverse.

| 15. SUBJECT TERMS |
|---|
| Media, Mass Media, Social Media, New Media, Grand Strategy, Information Operations, Character of War, CNN Effect |

| 16. SECURITY CLASSIFICATION OF: | | | 17. LIMITATION OF ABSTRACT | 18. NUMBER OF PAGES | 19a. NAME OF RESPONSIBLE PERSON |
|---|---|---|---|---|---|
| a. REPORT UU | b. ABSTRACT UU | c. THIS PAGE UU | UU | 40 | 19b. TELEPHONE NUMBER *(Include area code)* |

**Empire Maintenance in the Information Age:  Influence of Mediaverse on Strategy**

by

Lieutenant Colonel Christopher S. Lohr
United States Air Force

Dr. J. Sherwood McGinnis
Department of National Security and Strategy
Project Adviser

U.S. Army War College
CARLISLE BARRACKS, PENNSYLVANIA 17013

# Abstract

| | |
|---|---|
| Title: | Empire Maintenance in the Information Age:  Influence of Mediaverse on Strategy |
| Report Date: | March 2013 |
| Page Count: | 40 |
| Word Count: | 6,365 |
| Key Terms: | Media, Mass Media, Social Media, New Media, Grand Strategy, Information Operations, Character of War, CNN Effect |
| Classification: | Unclassified |

The proliferation of mobile Internet technology grants the average global citizen immediate access to information and the ability to posit opinions, i.e. influence, at near-real-time speed.  The amalgam of 24/7 news networks, mass media, the Internet, and social media (the mediaverse), coupled with mobile technology, influences strategy in three ways.  First, it is a national security challenge and opportunity.  Second, it influences the character of war.  Third, it is forcing an evolution of the strategic environment.  The successful strategic leader must be not just aware but au courant on the challenges and opportunities presented by the mediaverse.  Improved processes, tools, and education are required to adapt to mediaverse influencers.  The most significant systemic improvement is the addition of a robust strategic feedback loop in the strategy formulation model.  This can be accomplished by better integrating information operators into campaign planning and mission execution to surveil the mediaverse to assess content and on-going events to provide a robust assessment of the information environment.  Formal developmental education should expand current media training to include skillful reconnaissance of, and engagement in, the mediaverse.

**Empire Maintenance in the Information Age: Influence of Mediaverse on Strategy**

Wilkes College, Wilkes-Barre Pennsylvania, January 17, 1991. Three students returned from break a little early; they were the only ones in the campus dorms. On this night, the drinking games and laundry were put aside because they were glued to the television. They were watching the opening waves of OPERATION DESERT STORM play out live on CNN.

DESERT STORM was fought with unprecedented news coverage. This coverage was different than in previous wars. The message was not shaped by the United States government as it was in World War II, and reporters did not have to make their own way to the aftermath of a battle as they did in Vietnam. In DESERT STORM, reporters were embedded with the soldiers and the news cycle was 24 hours a day, 7 days a week. It was CNN's coming out party, the greatest media event in history![1] Reporters had access *and* mobility, and the Department of Defense held daily press briefings. The Pentagon carefully chose its spokesman, Lieutenant General Thomas Kelly, because he had experience with the media from the invasion of Panama and was blunt, humorous and down to earth. CNN presented images of the well-polished general verbally jousting with inquisitive reporters. These briefs were so popular and successful that they were parodied on Saturday Night Live.

Fast-forward 20 years to Sunday, May 1, 2011. A family in Waco Texas is watching the Philadelphia Phillies play the New York Mets at Citizens Bank Park in Philadelphia. The game is aired live on ESPN and this military family is tuned in because these teams represent a household rivalry. The game is tied at 1 in the top of the ninth inning when cheers of "U-S-A. U-S-A. U-S-A." break out across the stadium. As the cameras scan the crowd, America sees fans on their phones, while others are waving flags.  Back in Waco, one of the family members opens the Facebook app on her iPhone and discovers why the fans are cheering.  On the field in Philadelphia, the Phillies huddle on the mound, not understanding, not knowing what the fans do, that Osama bin Laden is dead.

Figure 1 – A Phillies fans learns of Osama bin Laden's death[2]

From CNN to social media, the world is getting smaller and more connected. "Social networking didn't start a revolution [that] Sunday night in Philadelphia.  But it did bring an entire stadium of people – and the nation – together in one single unifying moment."[3]

Empire Maintenance and the Information Age

Does the media carry influence in the strategic environment?  Since OPERATION DESERT STORM in 1991, 24/7 news networks exploded in number;

social media, enabled by cell phone technology, put information and the power to influence in almost everyone's hands. This research project initially addresses the "CNN Effect" because it provides a chronological, as well as anecdotal, starting point. However, the intent is to focus more on the influence of the Internet and social media rather than cable news networks. The term *mediaverse* is coined to allow the intellectual freedom of movement to maneuver within the realm of the television news networks, mass media, the Internet, and social media without bogging down in the details of the specific transfer medium. Particular attention to and recognition of the specific source or type of media is used as required to provide clarity or context.

This research project seeks to examine the influence of the mediaverse on strategy. The grand strategy of the United States from 1980 to the present, a period during which the United States emerged as the sole global superpower, is used to set the strategic context. The term *Empire Maintenance* is used to capture this strategy. Specifically this paper looks at the mediaverse 1) as both a national security challenge and an opportunity for the United States in the 21st Century; 2) and it's role in the theory of war and strategy; and 3) as a critical element, enabler, and process that defines the strategic environment in peace, conflict, and war.

Empire Maintenance

Grand strategy is the sectional chart national leaders use to navigate the turbulent airspace of the complex global environment; it defines our collective national purpose. It is based on national values and mores, and it is the determinant on how the nation will employ the instruments of power to preserve national existence and way of life. Grand strategy drives national policy and international engagement.

The concept of *empire maintenance* provides a contextual framework for United States grand strategy since 1980. The term, admittedly somewhat cynical in nature, is used intentionally to express the view that the preponderance of conflict for the United States in the late and post-cold war era consisted of wars of choice. The notable exception was the United States invasion of Afghanistan that began as a retaliatory military action for the attacks of 9/11.

Empire maintenance falls into the primacy framework of grand strategy. Just like primacy, it is characterized as an "active and assertive posture that reflects the offensive realists worldview of an international system characterized by ongoing power struggles."[4] Primacy requires significant forward presence across the globe, and the ability and willingness to use force in the pursuit of national interests. Thucydides expressed this sentiment when he wrote, "Right, as the world goes, is only in question between equals in power, while the strong do what they can and the weak suffer what they must."[5] For the United States, empire maintenance legitimizes challenging and checking potential political, military, or economic rivals and keeping plausible near-peer competitors from stifling American influence and dominance; a clear tendency of primacy.[6] This concept supports the thinking that use of force is a legitimate option to secure national interests, even in the absence of a direct threat. In other words, empire maintenance, just like primacy, may necessitate preventative war.[7]

The CNN Effect

In 1980, 52 American hostages remained captive in Iran. At home, *Star Wars: The Empire Strikes Back* and Blondie's *Call Me* topped the movie and music charts, the Philadelphia Phillies won the World Series, the number one threat to the United States was global thermonuclear war with the Soviet Union, and the Internet did not yet exist.[8]

4

CNN first raced across the airwaves in this year as well. Its constant news cycle let people get the news when they wanted it.[9] In sharp contrast to the major networks that only carried regimented morning, evening and late-night news, CNN brought current events programming to the consumer 24 hours a day. In those days it was, "a runty communications organization, with big ambitions and a small audience."[10] Today, CNN's staff of over 4000 people brings continuous news programming on multiple channels and the Internet in numerous languages across the United States and around the world.[11]

To the extent possible during the 1980s, CNN reporters covered America's small wars in Panama, Grenada, Libya, Lebanon, and elsewhere, along with their network colleagues. The difference between the two was that, because of its 24-hour news cycle, CNN was getting the story first, and repeating and updating it much more often. It was not long before CNN became a household name. As the channel's coverage and reach extended, so did its influence. The *CNN Effect* was born from this success and the associated success of other fledgling 24/7 news companies in the 1990s. This phenomenon extended the supposition that global, real-time media outlets like CNN have the ability to affect foreign policy and national response to crises.[12] Today the CNN Effect is subsumed by a broader *Internet effect* that challenges traditional thought about the relationships among media, foreign policy, and public opinion.

CNN founder Ted Turner said, "My main concern is to be a benefit to the world, to build up a global communications system that helps humanity come together."[13] His vision came true in ways he could not possibly have imagined. His idea of 24/7 news television spawned innumerable other news channels broadcasting from countries

5

across the globe in almost every language. These channels didn't just bring world news to America; they brought American news to the world, and along with it, various interpretations of America's activities abroad.

By the early days of the 21$^{st}$ century, the Internet connected homes worldwide. Shortly thereafter, cellular technology and smartphones introduced the Internet to countless mobile consumers across the globe. The 24/7 news cycle was taken to the next level by Web-based news content, which provide a nearly infinite variety of news products available at all times. The Internet allows more people to become part of the "culture of information."[14]

## Welcome to the Mediaverse

The plethora of 24/7 cable news networks have the power to inform, the Internet adds access and the power to inspire, and social media adds the power to enliven; collectively, the mediaverse has the power to move people both emotionally and to action. "As robust as the expansion of satellite television has been, it is nothing when compared to the growth of Internet-based media."[15] The Internet enables access to virtually limitless content, news, and ideas; it facilitates communication with individuals or the masses, next door or across the globe.[16] Add the mobility associated with cellular technology and smartphones and people now have instant access to information, ideas, and a means to communicate and rally. Thus, the mediaverse, the amalgamation of television news networks, mass media, the Internet, and social media, is a powerful influencer, limited only by the imagination and the will of those operating within it. A brief examination of each element is worthwhile to reinforce the concept of the mediaverse.

From CNN's launch in 1980, to the multitude of news channels across the globe today, 24/7 news channels are here to stay. A cursory review of the local television channel lineup reveals no less than 20 24/7 news channels available in high-definition, multiple languages, and tailored to the consumer's interests, be it, breaking news, business news, political news, sports news, or weather news.[17] As information becomes more available, consumers become increasingly astute and aware of the global environment. 24/7 news channels bring entertainment, sports, politics, or military actions, relentlessly to American households everyday.

Just as 24/7 news channels deliver news when people want it, the Internet delivers *everything* when people want it. This is a paramount feature in the "instant gratification" society of the United States today. The information resources of the world are available to anyone with access to the Internet, and almost everyone has access.

**Internet adoption, 1995-2011**

% of American adults (age 18+) who use the internet, over time. As of August 2011, 78% of adults use the internet.

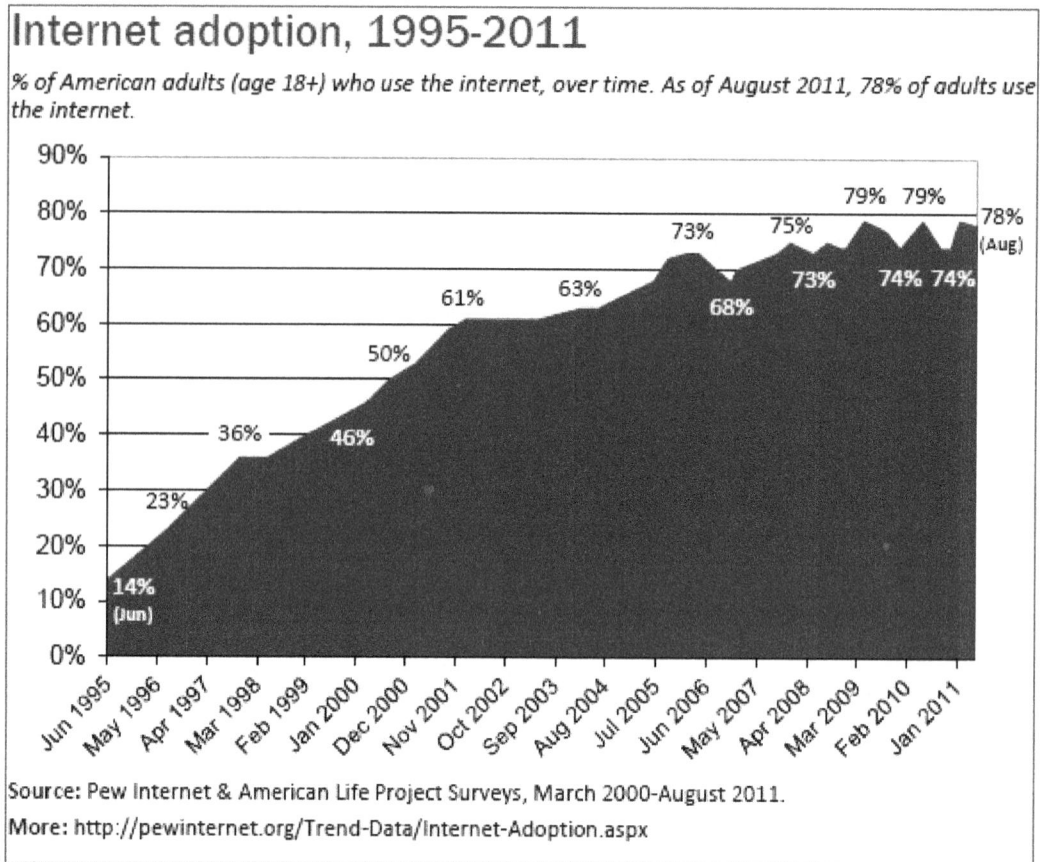

Source: Pew Internet & American Life Project Surveys, March 2000-August 2011.
More: http://pewinternet.org/Trend-Data/Internet-Adoption.aspx

Figure 2 – US Internet Adoption, 1995-2011[18]

"The Internet is for many the 21st century's newspaper. Arguably, the greatest change brought about by the Internet is a vast increase in the circulation of messages and meanings that make up agendas for the media, the public and government."[19] The Internet affords individuals access to information previously unavailable to them. It offers ways to communicate via email, chat, videoconference, etc., and it provides a forum for on-line collaboration, commerce, and opens the doorway to social media.

The consumer is not the only one leveraging the Internet. Those 24/7 news channels beaming into American homes have expanded their presence to include digital news websites, thereby easing access to ideas and information. Virtually every major news organization is moving towards interactive news because new communications

8

technology and the Internet accelerate the flow and global accessibility of news.[20]

Today the Internet experience is made more personal by enabling mobile technology

that allows users to bring the Internet with them.  Cellphones, smartphones, e-readers,

and tablets are commonplace among adult Americans.

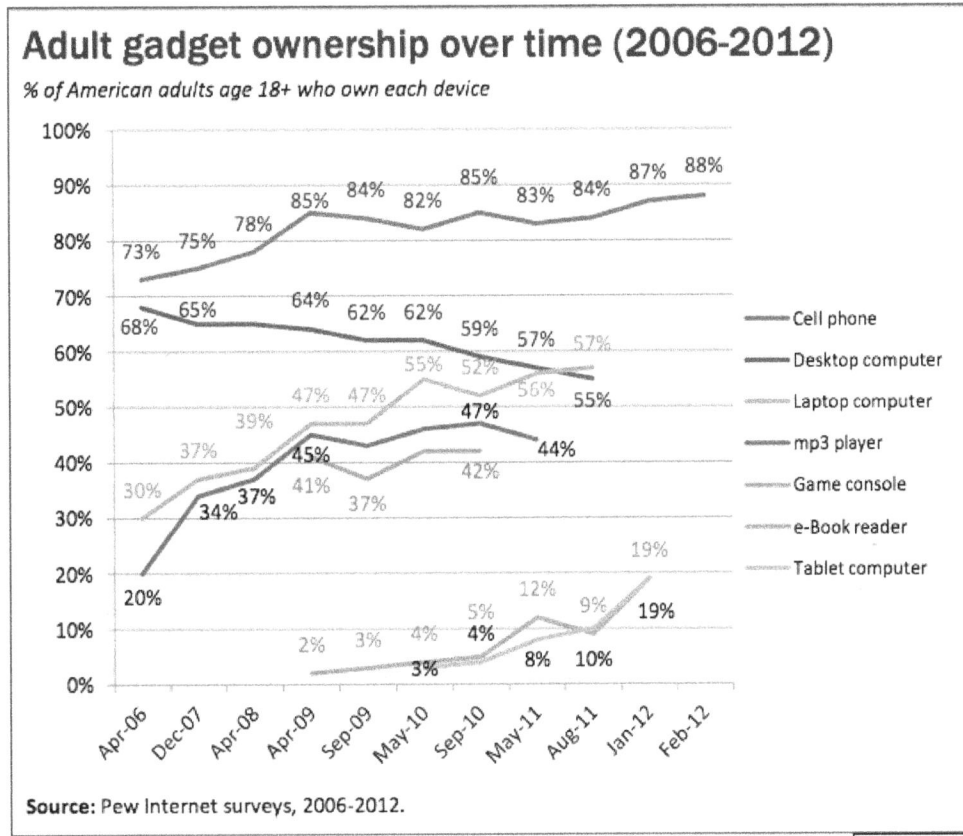

**Adult gadget ownership over time (2006-2012)**

*% of American adults age 18+ who own each device*

Source: Pew Internet surveys, 2006-2012.

Figure 3 – US Adult Gadget Ownership[21]

Social media sites such as Facebook, LinkedIn, Twitter, Instagram, Pinterest,

and Tumblr are connecting people with loved ones abroad and exposing them to

content beyond their individual sphere of influence.  Social media is an attractive petri

dish for ideas because the concepts of speed and transparency are intertwined.[22]  Of

interest is a look at what social media sites are most used by Americans:

Table 1 – US Social Media Users by Site[23]

| Who Uses Social Media | | | | | | |
|---|---|---|---|---|---|---|
| % of Internet users within each group who use the specific social media source identified un each column | | | | | | |
| | Facebook | LinkedIn | Twitter | Instagram | Pinterest | Tumblr |
| **All Internet Users (n=799)** | 66% | 20% | 16% | 12% | 12% | 5% |
| Men (n=393) | 63 | 21 | 17 | 11 | 5 | 4 |
| Woman (n=406) | 70 | 19 | 15 | 12 | 19 | 7 |
| **Age** | | | | | | |
| 18-29 (n=140) | 83 | 16 | 27 | 27 | 16 | 11 |
| 30-49 (n=224) | 72 | 25 | 15 | 8 | 12 | 4 |
| 50-64 (n=229) | 56 | 22 | 12 | 6 | 13 | 2 |
| 65+ (n=182) | 40 | 11 | 7 | 4 | 4 | 1 |
| **Annual Household Income** | | | | | | |
| Less than $30,000/yr (n=195) | 73 | 7 | 15 | 8 | 11 | 6 |
| $30,000 - $49,999 (n=156) | 75 | 20 | 14 | 14 | 8 | 6 |
| $50,000 - $74,999 (n=128) | 68 | 24 | 15 | 9 | 16 | 2 |
| $75,000+ (n=218) | 57 | 34 | 19 | 16 | 12 | 3 |
| **Education Level** | | | | | | |
| High school grad or less (n=238) | 73 | 7 | 12 | 8 | 8 | 3 |
| Some college (n=230) | 63 | 17 | 21 | 15 | 15 | 7 |
| College + (N=329) | 64 | 36 | 16 | 12 | 14 | 5 |

**Source:** Pew Research Center's Internet & American Life Project, Omnibus Survey, Aug. 2-5, 2012. N=1,005 adults ages 18 and older, including 405 interviews conducted on respondent's cell phone. The survey was conducted in English. Margin of error is +/-3.8 percentage points for internet users (n=799).

Clearly, the domestic audience is active and engaged in the mediaverse, and Americans are increasingly liberated from the Internet access points in their homes and offices by the availability of ever improving cellular, smartphone and tablet technologies. The American public is taking advantage of mobile access to Internet news and social media connections and associated content.

Table 2 – US Social Networking via Mobile Phone[24]

## Social Networking on Mobile Phones

*% of cell phone owners who use a social networking site on their phone*

| All cell phone owners (n=1,954) | 40% |
|---|---|
| Men (n=895) | 39 |
| Women (n=1,059) | 41 |
| **Age** | |
| 18-29 (n=340) | 67*** |
| 30-49 (n=562) | 50** |
| 50-64 (n=587) | 18* |
| 65+ (n=429) | 5 |
| **Race/ethnicity** | |
| White, Non-Hispanic (n=1,404) | 36 |
| Black, Non-Hispanic (n=234) | 48* |
| Hispanic (n=180) | 49* |
| **Annual household income** | |
| Less than $30,000/yr (n=447) | 38 |
| $30,000-$49,999 (n=316) | 40 |
| $50,000-$74,999 (n=272) | 48* |
| $75,000+ (n=538) | 45* |
| **Education level** | |
| No high school diploma (n=156) | 33 |
| High school grad (n=542) | 37 |
| Some College (n=490) | 42* |
| College + (n=752) | 43** |

Source: Pew Internet Spring Tracking Survey, March 15 – April 3, 2012. N=2,254 adults ages 18+. Interviews were conducted in English and Spanish and on landline and cell phones. Margin of error is +/- 3 percentage points for results based on cell phone owners.
* Statistically significant difference compared with others in the same grouping

The fascination with social media is not simply a US phenomenon; social networks are connecting people of all ages across the globe. The world is embracing the mediaverse in general, and social media in particular. The tools of the Information Age are changing every aspect of life on our planet, especially how people establish and maintain contact and share knowledge.[25] The by-product of information sharing is influence, and in this sense, the strategic ramifications of the networked, instant-access world are only marginally understood.  To paraphrase Larson and Livingston the media can affect strategy in different ways:  1) as a policy-agenda-setting agent; (2) as an impediment to the achievement of desired strategic goals; and (3) as an accelerant to strategic decision-making.[26]

Information Operations (IO)

This research project is about the speed, agility, and pervasiveness of social media and the mediaverse; it is not about "Strategic Communications" writ large.  For the military, the specific utility of this realm falls under *Information Operations*.  Joint Publication 3-13 (JP 3-13) defines Information Operations as,

> The integrated employment, during military operations, of information-related capabilities in concert with other lines of operation to influence, disrupt, corrupt, or usurp the decision-making of adversaries and potential adversaries while protecting our own.[27]

JP 3-13 aims to lay a foundation for the employment of the national instruments of power in the information environment.  The document defines this environment as, "the aggregate of individuals, organizations, and systems that collect, process, disseminate, or act on information."[28]  JP 3-13 is notable for two important reasons:  1) the fact that there is a joint publication defining information operations and its role in the battlespace signifies an awareness of the importance of the mediaverse as a domain; and 2) JP 3-13 prescribes a framework to include inform and influence activities in the Joint Operational Planning Process and the strategy formulation process.

Strategy Formulation

Strategy evolves from policy.  The civilian leaders of the United States lay the foundations for strategy development through various formal and informal means.  Formal mechanisms include things such as the National Security Strategy and the

National Defense Strategy; informal foundations are often derived from presidential speeches such as the State of the Union Address. These sources bound the problem for strategists by providing definition and policy objectives. The nation's military leaders then develop subordinate guidance and objectives to be used for planning. The National Military Strategy, signed out by the Chairman of the Joint Chiefs of Staff, is one such example. Military planners use this direction to develop theater strategies and, further down the chain, operational plans. While the particulars of the military planning process are beyond the scope of this paper, it is useful to understand the top-down nature of how strategy is crafted and translated to military objectives.

Before analysis of the influence of the mediaverse on strategy, it is necessary to set a contextual framework for discussion by first defining what is meant by *strategy*. Robert Dorff defined strategy as the relationship among ends, ways, and means.[29]

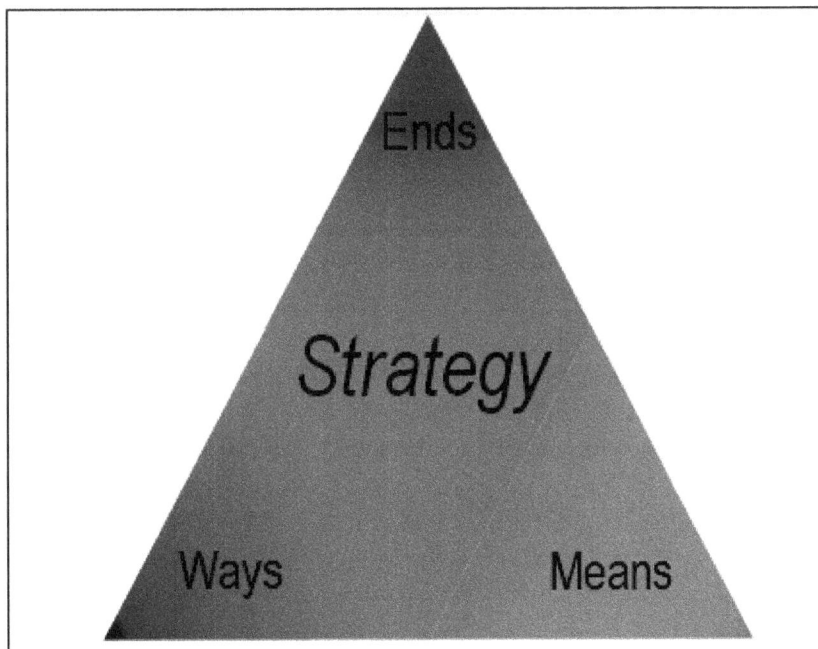

Figure 4 – Strategy is a function of Ends, Ways, and Means

Because strategy is a function of ends, ways, and means, it is important to have an accurate understanding of the terminology. Arthur Lykke developed the strategic components definitions below:

Table 3 - Strategic Components Defined[30]

| Strategy = Ends + Ways + Means. | |
|---|---|
| Component | Definition |
| Ends | Objectives towards which one strives |
| Ways | Course of action |
| Means | Instruments by which some end can be achieved |

The starting point for any strategy is the desired end-state. When crafting strategy, one assesses the environment, and then determines what that environment should look like in the future. This future state is known as the **ends**. This is typically the easiest portion to develop because it is quite often communicated in the documents highlighted above. In short, the ends define where you want to go, but not how to get there.

Knowing where to go is a good start, but it is necessary to determine how to get there. The **ways** describe the strategic approach to achieving the end-state, which is how resources will be applied to achieve the conditions desired.[31]

After determining where to go, and how to get there, it is still necessary to determine what tools or resources will be used to get there, these are known as the **means**. Means can be tangible, such as forces, equipment or money, or intangible such as the "will of the people."[32] The familiar national instruments of power, Diplomacy, Information, Military, Economics, or DIME, are the starting points in an assessment of available means.

The strategy formulation model in Figure 5 is a useful tool to help visualize these concepts. The model starts with national purpose and interests that are communicated through the strategy documents or presidential words and actions previously referenced. The interaction between ends, ways, and means is shown within the context of Strategy Formulation Process.

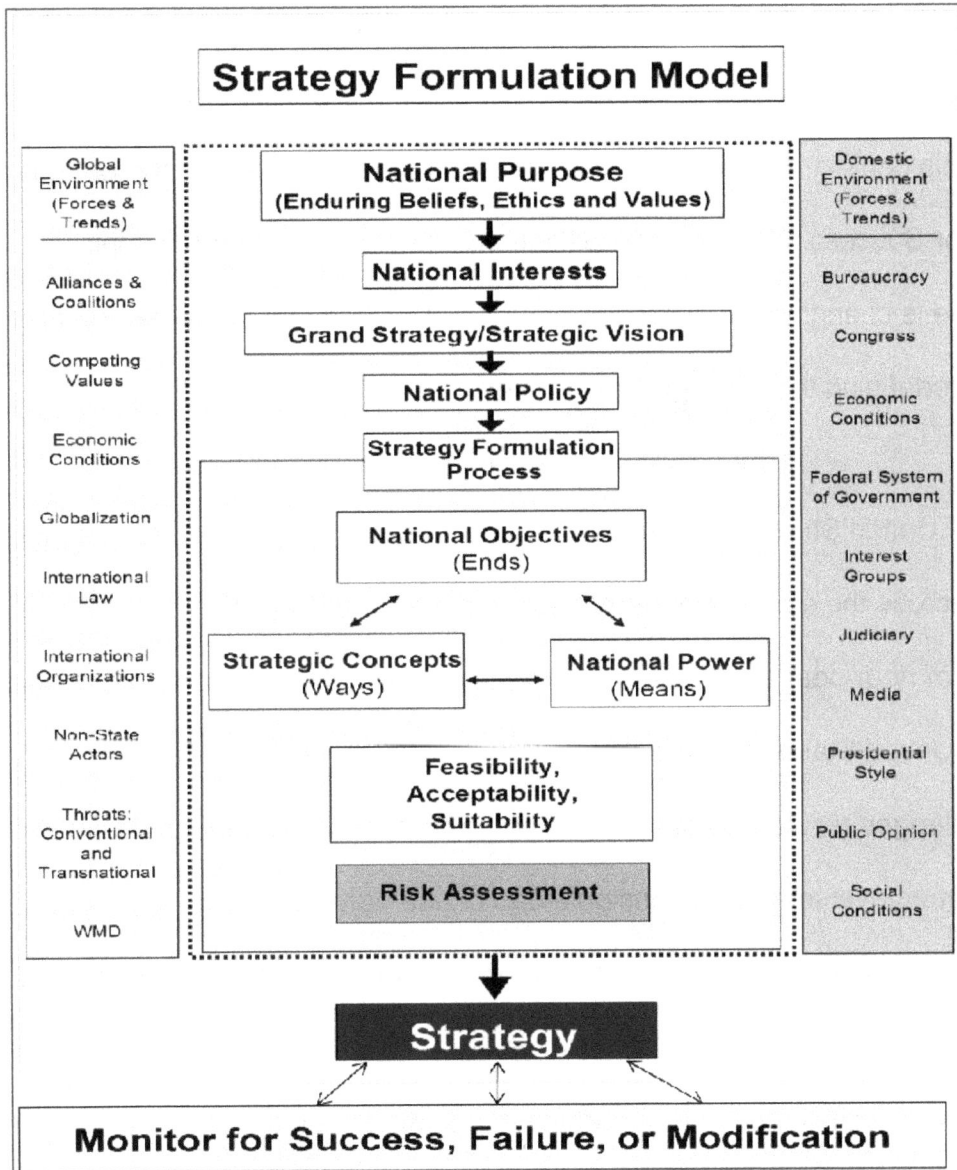

## Strategy Formulation Model

| Global Environment (Forces & Trends) | National Purpose (Enduring Beliefs, Ethics and Values) | Domestic Environment (Forces & Trends) |
| --- | --- | --- |

National Interests

Grand Strategy/Strategic Vision

National Policy

Strategy Formulation Process

National Objectives (Ends)

Strategic Concepts (Ways) — National Power (Means)

Feasibility, Acceptability, Suitability

Risk Assessment

Global Environment column:
- Alliances & Coalitions
- Competing Values
- Economic Conditions
- Globalization
- International Law
- International Organizations
- Non-State Actors
- Threats: Conventional and Transnational
- WMD

Domestic Environment column:
- Bureaucracy
- Congress
- Economic Conditions
- Federal System of Government
- Interest Groups
- Judiciary
- Media
- Presidential Style
- Public Opinion
- Social Conditions

**Strategy**

**Monitor for Success, Failure, or Modification**

Figure 5 - Strategy Formulation Model[33]

15

Of particular interest is the "National Power" block, or the means. As detailed above, instruments of power, or DIME, are assessed here. In general, the mediaverse falls under the informational element of power, but it can be used as a military asset as part of information operations. In either realm, it can be used as a tool (opportunity) for the United States. Unfortunately, it is likewise a threat or challenge to the United States if the enemy leverages the mediaverse and forces a reactive rather than proactive stance. This, unfortunately, is the position in which the United States quite often finds itself. In this context, the mediaverse can also fit as an element on the bottom block, "Monitor for Success, Failure, or Modification." The ambiguity and complexity of the mediaverse is changing the character of war and strategy (to some extent) and is therefore redefining the strategic environment.

Empire Maintenance in the Information Age

The United States faces increasing challenges as it maneuvers to secure its interests across the globe. Some of these challenges are physical, such as advances in weaponry of near-peer competitors. Some of these challenges are indirect, including a decline in United States prestige and economy over the first decade of the 21st century. Other challenges result from progress in communications technology. One example of this is the mediaverse and the tension it can cause between the government and those it governs, and between competing actors on the global stage. With respect to national security, the mediaverse introduces complexity to three specific areas: 1) it is both a national security challenge and opportunity; 2) it influences the character of war; and 3) it is forcing an evolution of the strategic environment.

## The Mediaverse as a National Security Challenge and Opportunity

The sheer speed and transparency of information flow is a key factor in its ability to influence actions and perceptions.[34] The mediaverse is a challenge and sometimes a liability because it may force a strategic hand or expedite the decision-making timeline resulting in adoption of a reactive posture. This reactive stance presents a challenge that must be recognized and transformed into opportunity. The mediaverse presents national security opportunities because it acts as a force enabler by allowing immediate messaging, and by association, influence or coercion, if executed correctly in a timely fashion.

A cursory review of key United States military operations since 1980 reveals a powerful United States political and military machine being matched and sometimes bested by emerging media outlets. Coming off the painful lessons of the Vietnam War and the media-fueled lack of popular support, President Jimmy Carter found himself between a rock and a hard place when Iranian students stormed the United States Embassy in Teheran, capturing and holding 52 Americans hostage. The sharp contrast between this crisis and the decade of fighting in Vietnam was that the people of the United States understood the situation and did not like it. Print and television media kept the story at the forefront, rightfully so, but in doing so, they applied unrelenting pressure on President Carter to attempt OPERATION EAGLE CLAW, the ill-fated military rescue attempt executed in late April of 1980.[35] This vignette, the first empire maintenance military action of the information age, laid the foundation for limited media access to the military for the remainder of the decade.

As a result of the pressure put on President Carter, and the dramatic operational failure in the Iranian desert, the media was in essence kept out of covering military

17

operations in Grenada in 1983 and Panama in 1989. However, a few enduring images such as the American medical student from Grenada kissing U.S. soil after landing at Andrews Air Force Base; and Manual Noriega holed up in the Vatican Embassy in Panama, helped convince senior military leaders that media access was a crucial part of strategic planning.[36] However, the fusion of strategic planning and media access is not without both benefit and risk.

The United States government was the recipient of beneficial media exposure during OPERATION RESTORE DEMOCRACY in 1994. As the military prepared to launch a joint invasion of Haiti to restore exiled President Aristide, the diplomatic and informational instruments of national power were hard at work. Former President Jimmy Carter led a behind the scenes negotiation team that included retired general and former Chairman of the Joint Chiefs of Staff, Colin Powell, and Senator Sam Nunn, to persuade Gen Raoul Cedras to cede his illegal control of the country, which he ultimately did. United States Army Lieutenant Colonel Margret H. Belknap writes, "Senator Nunn has often stated that live reports of American paratroopers lifting off from Fort Bragg enroute to invade Haiti directly led to General Cedras' decision to step down."[37]

In sharp contrast, the United States' strike on Libya in 1986, OPERATION EL DORADO CANYON, is a case where media coverage exacerbated military planning. This retaliatory airstrike against the regime of Muammar Qaddafi was the culmination of mounting tension after Libyan attacks on United States aircraft and personnel and the determination that Libya was behind terrorist attacks in West Berlin and on TWA flight 840.[38] As tension increased, media coverage, apparently fueled by high-level leaks in the White House, negated any hope of achieving the element of surprise.[39] The

intensity of the coverage drove allies away and nullified existing operational plans. Both

operations offer clear examples of media acting as a force multiplier or liability in

executing, strategy but not every military/mediaverse scenario is so unequivocally clear.

The United States' efforts in OPERATION DESERT SHIELD and DESERT

STORM in 1990 and 1991 are striking examples of the strategically positive and

negative influence carried by the media. The United States mission to liberate Kuwait

from Saddam Hussein "was the most widely and most swiftly reported war in history."[40]

Indeed, it is estimated that 600 million people across the globe watched the war on

television as it played out.[41] Media coverage at home led to overwhelming public

support for military operations and much of the beddown and human drama of the path

to war was broadcast on television and in print media. Americans understood and

supported why they were going to war. When operations shifted from deployment to

employment, the world watched live on CNN. In sharp contrast to the events in

Grenada and Panama, the media was granted access across the range of operations

from briefing rooms to foxholes. The military/media collaboration peaked with news

footage of the "Highway of Death." Unfortunately, the images of Iraqi forces in retreat

being picked off by U.S. Air Force A-10s left an unpalatable taste in the mouths of many

Americans. Ultimately the United States left Iraq having completed its basic objectives,

but without marching on to Baghdad. On this specific issue, Gen Colin Powell attributes

the decision not to take Baghdad as being a result of the Highway of Death footage on

CNN.[42] Thus, the CNN effect on strategy was born.

## The Mediaverse and the Character of War

"All wars consist of features that are unchangeable or constant, regardless of the era in which they are fought and those that are transitory or specific to a certain era. The first category makes up the war's "nature," while the second comprises its "character"."[43] The nature of war is characterized by those intangible universal constants that have puzzled man throughout the ages: psychological factors, irrationality, violence, hatred, uncertainty, friction, fear, danger, chance and luck.[44] It is here that the enduring lessons of Clausewitz, Thucydides, and Sun Tzu reign supreme. In contrast, the character of war is evolving, shaped by contemporary forces such as technology (e.g. drones), methodology (e.g. "Shock and Awe"), and other cultural influences (e.g. religion, economy, politics). Understanding the difference between the nature and character of war allows the intellectual maturity to analyze the influence of new or emerging information technologies (read mediaverse) on modern theories of war.

While the fundamental nature of war hasn't changed and won't change, the character of war is always changing.[45] United States Army Colonel Thomas D. Mayfield III described three areas of social media that affect or change the strategic environment: 1) speed/transparency with which information is passed; 2) ability to shape social dialogue because it bypasses traditional media; 3) and ability to organize without organizations.[46] While all three of these are valid, the first two in particular describe how the mediaverse can change the conduct and character of war.

On the night of March 27, 1999, an American F-117A Nighthawk stealth fighter was shot down over Kosovo. The Serbian military was quick to exploit the speed and transparency of the mediaverse by broadcasting images of the burning wreckage for

20

several hours before the Pentagon confirmed the shootdown.[47] Initial facts surrounding

the incident were clouded by Serbian misinformation about the engagement and the

fate of the crew.  The Serbs claimed two aircrew were captured, and other initial reports

incorrectly identified the pilot, who was rescued within hours, because the name on the

aircraft canopy in the video footage was different than the name of the pilot flying the

aircraft at the time.  Despite the confusion, intentional or otherwise, there was no

denying the fact that the United States had lost one of its top-secret jets.  The distinctive

design of the F-117 was easy to see in the photos and video of the wreckage

propagated by the Serbians.  The shootdown itself was a significant tactical coup for the

Serbians but their immediate propagandizing of the engagement was a more significant

strategic event.  This use of the media illustrated a perceived chink in the

technologically advanced armor of the Air Force and it put the United States in a

reactionary mode in the press.

The F-117 shootdown offers a strong example of the ability of mass media to get

in front of the political narrative.  Since that event in 1999, the mediaverse, by virtue of

the Internet and cellular technology, has expanded to influence more people, quicker

than ever before.  If television news channels radically altered the way war is presented,

the Internet opened Pandora's box.  As the proliferation of the Internet usurped the

influence of television, the global political and social environment expanded and grew

more interconnected.[48] Social media in particular allows the bypassing of traditional

media to help shape a perception.[49] This was evident on the part of both Hamas and the

Israeli Defense Force in October of 2012.

The mediaverse became a battleground when Israel and Hamas faced off on Twitter and YouTube in the world's first social media war.[50] Israel announced the start of OPERATION PILLAR OF DEFENSE via Twitter. As the conflict escalated, both sides waged war in Gaza and the mediaverse by posting videos, pictures, propaganda, and Twitter taunts in an effort to reach and influence the masses directly. The ethical merits of this type of cyber war are debated but it is clear that both combatants viewed social media as an opportunity to be exploited. The mediaverse has always been part of the operating environment but the 2012 Israel/Hamas fight differs from previous conflicts because the it was the first time the world saw "the institutions heading over to the medium of the witnesses and participants."[51]

Figure 6 – IDF Spokesman Announces OPERATION PILLAR OF DEFENSE[52]

Similarly, OPERATION ENDURING FREEDOM presented a phenomenal spectrum of warfighting technology with the United States on one end and the Taliban and al Qaeda on the other.  Indeed, as disparate as their weapon systems were, so was the recognition by al Qaeda of the mediaverse as a weapon of influence compared to the United States.  When U.S. forces attacked in late 2001, a Pakistani journalist on the scene wrote that while retreating from attack, "every second al Qaeda member was carrying a laptop computer along with his Kalashnikov."[53]  In contrast to the Israeli Defense Force's, and al Qaeda's contemporary active engagement in the mediaverse, the United States is wary and unsteady in its relationship with all forms of media.

The Mediaverse and the Strategic Environment

Just as the character of war is changing, the mediaverse is forcing an evolution of the strategic environment.  James Jay Carafano captured this in his book, *Wiki at War*, when he wrote,

> War in the real world is not limited to battlefields.  All conflicts cross every aspect of human activity.  Studying real war means looking at the economic, cultural, legal, social, and military dimensions of competition.  It means delving into how social networks and conflict play out on the broad vista of human affairs from the foxhole to the home front.[54]

Social media and the Internet make it easy, cheap, and safe to initiate contact with a large number of people.[55]  As a result, the transforming strategic environment is more challenging than ever in three particular ways:  1) the mediaverse enables immediate public visibility/exposure; 2) the mediaverse offers anonymity and therefore questionable credibility; and 3) the mediaverse facilitates mass collaboration and the impetus to rally.

The mediaverse enables immediate public awareness and scrutiny of strategic decisions and military operations as they unfold.[56]  There is no respite in today's

23

operational environment and the strategic leader must therefore be fully engaged at all times. Strategic leaders and warfighters must learn to make real-time decisions within the context of a complex dynamic environment that can be immediately visible to virtually anyone.[57] This environment invites not just public exposure but it may even compel intervention at the highest levels of government.

Lieutenant Colonel Belknap aptly characterized the phenomena and response of tactical actions having strategic consequences.

> The strategic leader and operational commander must consider the impact that information availability has on command and control...a valid concern is that the National Command Authority (NCA), as a result of the CNN effect, will have the capability and desire to micromanage the war. In a CNN War where the NCA is held accountable for tactical actions by a public media in real time, the NCA may feel compelled to become more involved as the situation develops.[58]

The mediaverse not only complicates executing strategy, it offers anonymity that can seed questions of credibility. Information and ideas gain momentum in the mediaverse with such rapidity and in such complex ways, it is impossible to identify or gauge the authority of a given source.[59] In addition to the reality that adjudicating fact from fiction is time-consuming, the speed of information transfer across the mediaverse can make truth irrelevant. If an adversary can spin a circumstance before truth is propagated, the strategic leader will be forced to spend considerable energy to right the story. There is no guarantee that the truth will ever catch up, thereby becoming irrelevant. In addition to offering anonymity, the extensive numbers of people in cyberspace and virtual worlds provide a degree of security.[60]

Anonymity and security further complicate the strategic environment because it can enable unintended collaboration and collective action. The mediaverse is fostering "the emergence of a visually-oriented, ideologically impulsive Internet culture with the means to rapidly and collectively plan and act."[61] This characteristic facilitates an evolving and dynamic operational environment that adds complexity to the strategic and operational environment.

## Conclusions

Empire maintenance in the information age is increasingly challenged by the speed, agility, and pervasiveness of the mediaverse and its influence on strategy. As such, the mediaverse is both a challenge and an opportunity to national security. It is changing the character of war, and is transforming the nature of the strategic environment.

With respect to challenge and opportunity, James Rubin, chief spokesman for the State Department during President Clinton's second administration, captured the dichotomy of the CNN effect when Keith Porter interviewed him on the radio program, *Common Ground*, on July 14, 1998. Regarding the challenge of responding to world events solely because they are broadcast on TV, he said, "The short answer is yes, there is a greater urgency to respond," but he also added, "The harder question is does it change your response."[62] While he did not specifically address the latter, he did highlight the opportunity presented by the media:

> When you don't have pictures and you don't have real-time information
> about something that's going on in the world, it's often much more difficult
> to convince people that something matters...so to the extent that it makes,
> brings to bear public opinion in a way that is activist, generally speaking
> that's a good thing.[63]

It is the responsibility of the strategic leader to manage the challenges and exploit the opportunities presented by the mediaverse in conflict. Military commanders must learn to see the media as potential allies rather than as enemies.[64] The successful strategic leader must be not just aware but *au courant* on the challenges and

25

opportunities presented by the multitude of 24/7 news channels and social media. In an era where wars can be won or lost in the mediaverse or the battlefield, strategic leaders and warfighters must be proactive and innovative in dealing with the media.[65]

The mediaverse is changing the character of war. Because media coverage of tactical events has strategic implications, war is much more visible and public than ever before.[66] The speed and transparency of the mediaverse is blurring the lines between the actors and the audience, making war more easily accessible and deliverable; it is becoming an audience-participation event. The conflict between Israel and Hamas in October of 2012 is a perfect example. This aspect of war requires improved processes and tools to manage it.

Just as the character of war is changing, the mediaverse is forcing a transformation of the strategic environment. The reality today is that technology enables almost instant access to any event to any person. Short of censorship, there is nothing that can be done about this directly. Furthermore, the culture of the Internet and new media is also changing the traditional notion of credibility.[67] However, it may be possible to *mitigate* risk in both of these areas through education and the purposeful exploitation of the mediaverse.

## Recommendations

How can the effectiveness of a strategic leader be improved in an environment of a pervasive mediaverse? The first step is to understand and appreciate that the mediaverse can, in fact, influence strategy. Once that premise is accepted, it is possible to mitigate that influence through conceptual improvements to strategy formulation; a doctrinal improvement to planning and execution; and through improved education and training.

The most significant systemic improvement that can be made is the addition of a robust strategic feedback loop during the development and execution of strategy. The Strategy Formulation Model (Figure 5) includes a block entitled "Monitor for Success, Failure, or Modification." This concept needs to evolve to a more assertive "Strategic Feedback Loop" that encourages active *environmental scanning and maneuvering* at the strategic level to adapt to mediaverse influencers. This novel competency encompasses the skills of environmental scanning, envisioning, skillful coordination and cross-cultural savvy. In short, "environmental scanning and maneuvering" is interpreting the environment, culling the essential factors or requirements, and acting across organizational or national bounds, as appropriate, to achieve the desired effect. This active and iterative process will provide the illumination necessary to develop and evaluate an effective strategic flight plan, and to provide course corrections as required.

The backbone of a robust strategic feedback loop is the integration of information operators into strategy formulation. In general, information operators are public affairs specialists, and practitioners of military information support operations and inform and influence activities. At the theater and operational level, information operators must be truly integrated into not just planning, but also mission execution. At present, the doctrinal assessment of IO and the information environment is focused on the performance and effectiveness of activities in order to provide feedback to modify activities that *achieve desired results*.[68] There must be a more robust assessment of the information environment that analyzes: 1) activities that *failed* to achieve desired results in order to modify operations, and more importantly; 2) enemy activities in the mediaverse that shape local perceptions and popular support. These more difficult

27

cognitive effects are typically analyzed through the Intelligence function rather than the IO function. This limits accessibility to information and analysis of specific IO objectives. The solution is to employ information operators to surveil the mediaverse to assess content and on-going events to develop not only actionable responses, but also proactive messaging.

Finally, military and civilian education, at all levels, should include some content to increase awareness of the opportunities and pitfalls associated with the mediaverse. Pre-deployment training for all expeditionary forces should reinforce this understanding with the aim to prevent, or at least minimize, a tactical environment that enables the "strategic corporal" to inadvertently take action that may be counter to strategic objectives. Mid and senior level developmental education programs should expand current public affairs training to include skillful reconnaissance and engagement in the mediaverse. This should be a core institutional learning objective and not merely an elective offering.

Properly cultivated, understood, and exploited, the mediaverse is a powerful weapon in the arsenal of war but it does not distinguish between friend and foe, belligerent or bystander. It is essential to dominate in this realm because as James Jay Carafano explains, "As an instrument of war, the power of mass mobilization through social networks represents a potentially dominant competitive advantage."[69]

## Endnotes

[1] Hudson, Miles, and John Stanier. 1998. *War and the Media: A Random Searchlight*. New York: New York University Press, 209.

[2] Dustin Schoof, "Philadelphia Phillies Fans Learn of Osama bin Laden's Death Through the Internet," The Express-Times (from lehighvalleylive.com), 2 May 2011,

http://www.lehighvalleylive.com/sports/index.ssf/2011/05/philadelphia_phillies_fans_lea.html. (accessed January 12, 2013)

   [3] Ibid.

   [4] Tami Davis Biddle, "Grand Strategy: Art of the Possible or Impossible Art?". U.S. Army War College, Department of National Security and Strategy. Readings in National Security Policy and Strategy. Carlisle Barracks, PA: 2012, Section II, 74.

   [5] Robert B. Strassler, ed., *The Landmark Thucydides: A Comprehensive Guide to the Peloponnesian War* ( New York: The Free Press, 1996), 352.

   [6] Ibid., 74.

   [7] Ibid., 75.

   [8] Bryan Perry, "From Reagan to Obama, How We Have Changed as a Nation." CNN.com, 26 Jan 13, http://www.cnn.com/2013/01/26/politics/infographic-reaganobama/index.html?hpt=hp_c2 (accessed January 26, 2013).

   [9] Seib, Philip M. 2008. *The al Jazeera Effect: How the New Global Media are Reshaping World Politics.* Washington, D.C: Potomac Books, xii.

   [10] Arnett, Peter. 1994. *Live from the battlefield: From Vietnam to Baghdad: 35 Years in the World's War Zones.* New York: Simon & Schuster, 322.

   [11] http://www.cnn.com/about/ (accessed 26 Jan 13).

   [12] Larson, James F., and Foreign Policy Association. 2004. The Internet and foreign policy. Vol. no. 325. New York: Foreign Policy Association, 6.

   [13] Seib, *The al Jazeera Effect*, 2.

   [14] Ibid., xii.

   [15] Ibid., 47.

   [16] Ibid., 8.

   [17] Comcast xfinity Channel Lineup for Chambersburg/Shippensburg (PA), 1 Apr 12.

   [18] Zickuhr, Kathryn and Smith, Aaron, "Digital Differences," Pew Internet & American Life Project, 13 Apr 12, http://pewinternet.org/~/media//Files/Reports/2012/PIP_Digital_differences_041312.pdf (accessed January 27, 2013), 4.

   [19] Larson, *The Internet and Foreign Policy*, 9.

   [20] Ibid., 52.

[21] Zickuhr, Smith, and Aaron, Digital Differences, 14.

[22] Thomas D. Mayfield III, *The Impact of Social Media on the Nature of Conflict, and a Commander's Strategy for Social Media*, Senior Service College Fellowship Civilian Research Project (Carlisle Barracks, PA: U.S. Army War College, April 29, 2010), 12.

[23] Rainie, Lee, Brenner, Joanna and Purcell, Kristin, "Photos and Video as Social Currency On-line," Pew Internet & American Life Project, 13 Sep 12, http://pewinternet.org/~/media//Files/Reports/2012/PIP_OnlineLifeinPictures_PDF.pdf (accessed January 27, 2013), compilation of data on pages 10-15.

[24] Brenner, Joanna, "Pew Internet: Social Networking (full detail)," Pew Internet & American Life Project, 13 Nov 12, http://pewinternet.org/Commentary/2012/March/Pew-Internet-Social-Networking-full-detail.aspx# (accessed January 27, 2013).

[25] Carafano, James Jay. 2012. *Wiki at War: Conflict in a Socially Networked World*. College Station: Texas A&M University Press, 4.

[26] Larson, *The Internet and Foreign Policy*, 10.

[27] US Joint Chiefs of Staff, *Information Operations*, Joint Publication 3-13 (Washington, DC: US Joint Chiefs of Staff, 27 November, 2012) http://www.defenseinnovationmarketplace.mil/resources/12102012_io1.pdf, GL-3. (accessed February 24, 2013)

[28] JP 3-13, *Information Operations*, vii.

[29] Robert H. Dorff, "A Primer in Strategy Development," in U.S. Army War College, Guide to Strategy, Joseph R. Cerami and James F. Holcomb Jr., eds. (Carlisle Barracks, PA: US Army War College, Strategic Studies Institute, February 2001), 11.

[30] Arthur F. Lykke, Jr., "Toward an Understanding of Military Strategy," in U.S. Army War College, Guide to Strategy, Joseph R. Cerami and James F. Holcomb Jr., eds. (Carlisle Barracks, PA: US Army War College, Strategic Studies Institute, February 2001), 179.

[31] US Army War College, Department of Military Strategy, Planning, and Operations, Campaign Planning Handbook (Carlisle Barracks, PA: US Army War College, Academic Year 2013), 46.

[32] H. Richard Yarger, "Toward a Theory of Strategy:  Art Lykke and the U.S. Army War College Strategy Model," in US Army War College Guide to National Security Issues, Vol. I: Theory of War and Strategy, ed. J. Boone Bartholomees, Jr. (Carlisle Barracks, PA: U.S. Army War College, Strategic Studies Institute, June 2012), 49.

[33] US Army War College, Department of National Security and Strategy, National Security Policy and Strategy Course Directive and Reader (Carlisle Barracks, PA:  US Army War College, Academic Year 2013), 4.

[34] Mayfield III, *The Impact of Social Media*, 13.

[35] Hudson and Stanier. *War and the Media*, 316.

[36] Hudson and Stanier. *War and the Media*, 199, 207.

[37] Margaret H. Belknap, *The CNN Effect: Strategic Enabler or Operational Risk?*, Strategy Research Project (Carlisle Barracks, PA: U.S. Army War College, March 30, 2001), 15.

[38] Gregory Ball, "U.S. Air Force Fact Sheet: OPERATION EL DORADO CANYON," undated, http://www.afhso.af.mil/topics/factsheets/factsheet.asp?id=18650 (accessed February 18, 2013)

[39] Walter J. Boyne, "El Dorado Canyon," March 1999, http://www.airforce-magazine.com/MagazineArchive/Documents/1999/March%201999/0399canyon.pdf, 59. (accessed February 18, 2013)

[40] Hudson and Stanier. *War and the Media*, 209.

[41] Hudson and Stanier. *War and the Media*, 224.

[42] Powell, Colin L., and Joseph E. Persico. 1995. *My American Journey: An autobiography.* New York: Random House, 519-522.

[43] Milan Vego, "On Military Theory," *Joint Force Quarterly*, no. 62 (3rd Quarter, 2011): 64. http://www.ndu.edu/press/military-theory.html (accessed August 23, 2012)

[44] Ibid., 64.

[45] Paul Van Riper and Willis, Scott, edited by Vlack, A., and Tyson, P. "The Immutable Nature of War." May 4, 2004. PBS Nova Interview. http://www.pbs.org/wgbh/nova/military/immutable-nature-war.html (accessed September 23, 2012)

[46] Mayfield III, *The Impact of Social Media*, 10.

[47] NATO *Loses First Plane*, BBC News, 28 Mar 99, http://news.bbc.co.uk/2/hi/europe/306091.stm . (accessed February 23, 2013)

[48] Seib, *The al Jazeera Effect*, 7.

[49] Mayfield III, *The Impact of Social Media*, 10.

[50] The World's First Social Media War: Israel v. Hamas. Chatham, United States, Chatham: Newstex, 2012, http://search.proquest.com/docview/1179650641?accountid=4444. (accessed December 1, 2012)

[51] Ibid.

[52] https://twitter.com/AvitalLeibovich. (accessed February 18, 2013)

[53] Seib, *The al Jazeera Effect*, 102.

[54] Carafano, *Wiki at War*, 12.

[55] Steven Metz, "The Internet, New Media, and the Evolution of Insurgency," *Parameters* XLII, no. 3 (Autumn 2012): 84.

[56] Belknap, *The CNN Effect,* 1.

[57] Belknap, *The CNN Effect,* 13.

[58] Belknap, *The CNN Effect,* 14.

[59] Metz, "The Internet," 84.

[60] Ibid., 85.

[61] Brian Petit, "Social Media and UW," Special Warfare 25, no. 2 (April-June 2012):26.

[62] James Rubin interview by Keith Porter. "Media vs Military." Common Ground. July 14, 1998. http://commongroundradio.org/transcpt/98/9828.html. (accessed December 2, 2012).

[63] Ibid.

[64] Hudson and Stanier. *War and the Media*, 320.

[65] Belknap, *The CNN Effect,* 14.

[66] US Army War College Guest Speaker, AY2013.

[67] Metz, "The Internet," 84.

[68] JP 3-13, *Information Operations*, IV-8.

[69] Carafano, *Wiki at War*, 4.

# NOTABLE PASSAGES

*The AI was asked to identify the most interesting, complex, quotable, or famous passage of less than 150 words on each page. Pages without qualifying passages are omitted.*

| | |
|---|---|
| | *"Today, the information age has created a new battlefield, one that exists in the virtual realm of the mediaverse. This mediaverse is a complex and interconnected network of information, communication, and influence. It is a battleground where ideas, narratives, and perceptions are fought over, shaping the strategic landscape of nations and empires. In this new era, maintaining an empire requires not only physical force and military might, but also the ability to control and manipulate information. The power to shape narratives and control the flow of information has become a crucial aspect of modern warfare and statecraft. As Sun Tzu famously said, 'All warfare is based on deception.' In the information age, this deception takes on new forms, as disinformation campaigns, propaganda, and cyber attacks become powerful tools in the hands of those who seek to gain advantage in the mediaverse. The ability to navigate and exploit this virtual battlefield will determine the success or failure of empires in the 21st century."* |
| | *"The successful strategic leader must be not just aware but au courant on the challenges and opportunities presented by the mediaverse. Improved processes, tools, and education are required to adapt to mediaverse influencers. The most significant systemic improvement is the addition of a robust strategic feedback loop in the strategy formulation model. This can be accomplished by better integrating information operators into campaign planning and mission execution to surveil the mediaverse to assess content and on-going events to provide a robust assessment of the information environment. Formal developmental education should expand current media training to include skillful reconnaissance of, and engagement in, the mediaverse."* |
| 1 | *"DESERT STORM was fought with unprecedented news coverage. This coverage was different than in previous wars. The message was not shaped by the United States government as it was in World War II, and reporters did not have to make their own way to the aftermath of a battle as they did in Vietnam. In DESERT STORM, reporters were embedded with the soldiers and the news cycle was 24 hours a day, 7 days a week. It was CNN's coming out party, the greatest media event in history!"* |
| 2 | *"From CNN to social media, the world is getting smaller and more connected. 'Social networking didn't start a revolution [that] Sunday night in Philadelphia. But it did bring an entire stadium of people, and the nation, together in one single unifying moment.'"* |

| 3 | *"Grand strategy is the sectional chart national leaders use to navigate the turbulent airspace of the complex global environment; it defines our collective national purpose. It is based on national values and mores, and it is the determinant on how the nation will employ the instruments of power to preserve national existence and way of life. Grand strategy drives national policy and international engagement."* |
|---|---|
| 4 | *"For the United States, empire maintenance legitimizes challenging and checking potential political, military, or economic rivals and keeping plausible near-peer competitors from stifling American influence and dominance; a clear tendency of primacy."* |
| 5 | *"The CNN Effect was born from this success and the associated success of other fledgling 24/7 news companies in the 1990s. This phenomenon extended the supposition that global, real-time media outlets like CNN have the ability to affect foreign policy and national response to crises."* |
| 6 | *"The plethora of 24/7 cable news networks have the power to inform, the Internet adds access and the power to inspire, and social media adds the power to enliven; collectively, the mediaverse has the power to move people both emotionally and to action."* |
| 7 | *"A cursory review of the local television channel lineup reveals no less than 20 24/7 news channels available in high-definition, multiple languages, and tailored to the consumer,'interests, be it, breaking news, business news, political news, sports news, or weather news."* |
| 8 | *‚ÄúThe Internet is for many the 21st century's newspaper. Arguably, the greatest change brought about by the Internet is a vast increase in the circulation of messages and meanings that make up agendas for the media, the public and government.‚Äù* |
| 9 | *"Social media is an attractive petri dish for ideas because the concepts of speed and transparency are intertwined."* |
| 10 | *"The American public is taking advantage of mobile access to Internet news and social media connections and associated content."* |
| 11 | *"The tools of the Information Age are changing every aspect of life on our planet, especially how people establish and maintain contact and share knowledge."* |
| 12 | *"The fact that there is a joint publication defining information operations and its role in the battlespace signifies an awareness of the importance of the mediaverse as a domain; and JP 3-13 prescribes a framework to include inform and influence activities in the Joint Operational Planning Process and the strategy formulation process."* |
| 13 | *"Before analysis of the influence of the mediaverse on strategy, it is necessary to set a contextual framework for discussion by first defining what is meant by strategy. Robert Dorff defined strategy as the relationship among ends, ways, and means."* |
| 14 | *"The starting point for any strategy is the desired end-state. When crafting strategy, one assesses the environment, and then determines what that environment should look like in the future. This future state is known as the ends. This is typically the easiest portion to develop because it is quite often communicated in the documents highlighted above. In short, the ends define where you want to go, but not how to get there."* |

| 15 | *"The strategy formulation model in Figure 5 is a useful tool to help visualize these concepts."* |
|---|---|
| 16 | *"The ambiguity and complexity of the mediaverse is changing the character of war and strategy (to some extent) and is therefore redefining the strategic environment."* |
| 17 | *"The mediaverse is a challenge and sometimes a liability because it may force a strategic hand or expedite the decision-making timeline resulting in adoption of a reactive posture. This reactive stance presents a challenge that must be recognized and transformed into opportunity."* |
| 18 | *"Senator Nunn has often stated that live reports of American paratroopers lifting off from Fort Bragg enroute to invade Haiti directly led to General Cedras' decision to step down.* |
| 19 | *"The United States' efforts in OPERATION DESERT SHIELD and DESERT STORM in 1990 and 1991 are striking examples of the strategically positive and negative influence carried by the media. The United States mission to liberate Kuwait from Saddam Hussein 'was the most widely and most swiftly reported war in history.' Indeed, it is estimated that 600 million people across the globe watched the. war on television as it played out. Media coverage at home led to overwhelming public support for military operations and much of the beddown and human drama of the path to war was broadcast on television and in print media. Americans understood and supported why they were going to war. When operations shifted from deployment to employment, the world watched live on CNN. In sharp contrast to the events in Grenada and Panama, the media was granted access across the range of operations from briefing rooms to foxholes. The military/media collaboration peaked with news footage of the 'Highway of Death.'* |
| 20 | *"While the fundamental nature of war hasn't changed and won't change, the character of war is always changing."* |
| 21 | *"The F-117 shootdown offers a strong example of the ability of mass media to get in front of the political narrative. Since that event in 1999, the mediaverse, by virtue of the Internet and cellular technology, has expanded to influence more people, quicker than ever before. If television news channels radically altered the way war is presented, the Internet opened Pandora's box. As the proliferation of the Internet usurped the influence of television, the global political and social environment expanded and grew more interconnected."* |
| 22 | *"The mediaverse became a battleground when Israel and Hamas faced off on Twitter and YouTube in the world's first social media war."* |
| 23 | *"Just as the character of war is changing, the mediaverse is forcing an evolution of the strategic environment. James Jay Carafano captured this in his book, Wiki at War, when he wrote, War in the real world is not limited to battlefields. All conflicts cross every aspect of human activity. Studying real war means looking at the economic, cultural, legal, social, and military dimensions of competition. It means delving into how social networks and conflict play out on the broad vista of human affairs from the foxhole to the home front."* |
| 24 | *"The mediaverse not only complicates executing strategy, it offers anonymity that can seed questions of credibility. Information and ideas gain momentum in the mediaverse with such rapidity and in such complex ways, it is impossible to identify* |

*or gauge the authority of a given source. In addition to the reality that adjudicating fact from fiction is time-consuming, the speed of information transfer across the mediaverse can make truth irrelevant. If an adversary can spin a circumstance before truth is propagated, the strategic leader will be forced to spend considerable energy to right the story. There is no guarantee that the truth will ever catch up, thereby becoming irrelevant. In addition to offering anonymity, the extensive numbers of people in cyberspace and virtual worlds provide a degree of security."*

25    *"With respect to challenge and opportunity, James Rubin, chief spokesman for the State Department during President Clinton's second administration, captured the dichotomy of the CNN effect when Keith Porter interviewed him on the radio program, Common Ground, on July 14, 1998. Regarding the challenge of responding to world events solely because they are broadcast on TV, he said, 'The short answer is yes, there is a greater urgency to respond,' but he also added, 'The harder question is does it change your response.' While he did not specifically address the latter, he did highlight the opportunity presented by the media: When you don't have pictures and you don't have real-time information about something that's 'going on in the world, it's often much more difficult to convince people that something matters. Also o the extent that it makes, brings to bear public opinion in a way that is activist, generally speaking that,'a good thing."*

26    *"The mediaverse is changing the character of war. Because media coverage of tactical events has strategic implications, war is much more visible and public than ever before. The speed and transparency of the mediaverse is blurring the lines between the actors and the audience, making war more easily accessible and deliverable; it is becoming an audience-participation event."*

27    *"The most significant systemic improvement that can be made is the addition of a robust strategic feedback loop during the development and execution of strategy. The Strategy Formulation Model (Figure 5) includes a block entitled 'Monitor for Success, Failure, or Modification.' This concept needs to evolve to a more assertive 'Strategic Feedback Loop' that encourages active environmental scanning and maneuvering at the strategic level to adapt to mediaverse influencers. This novel competency encompasses the skills of environmental scanning, envisioning, skillful coordination and cross-cultural savvy. In short, 'environmental scanning and maneuvering' is interpreting the environment, culling the essential factors or requirements, and acting across organizational or national bounds, as appropriate, to achieve the desired effect. This active and iterative process will provide the illumination necessary to develop and evaluate an effective strategic flight plan, and to provide course corrections as required."*

28    *"Properly cultivated, understood, and exploited, the mediaverse is a powerful weapon in the arsenal of war but it does not distinguish between friend and foe, belligerent or bystander. It is essential to dominate in this realm because as James Jay Carafano explains, 'As an instrument of war, the power of mass mobilization through social networks represents a potentially dominant competitive advantage.'"*

www.ingramcontent.com/pod-product-compliance
Lightning Source LLC
Chambersburg PA
CBHW081203270326
41930CB00014B/3281